YOU CHOOSE BOOKS

HADES
AND THE
UNDERWORLD

AN INTERACTIVE MYTHOLOGICAL ADVENTURE

by Blake Hoena
illustrated by Nadine Takvorian

Consultant: Dr. Laurel Bowman
Department of Greek and Roman Studies
University of Victoria
Victoria, BC, Canada

CAPSTONE PRESS
a capstone imprint

You Choose Books are published by Capstone Press,
1710 Roe Crest Drive, North Mankato, Minnesota 56003
www.mycapstone.com

Library of Congress Cataloging-in-Publication Data
Names: Hoena, B. A., author.
Title: Hades and the underworld : an interactive mythological adventure /
by Blake Hoena.
Description: North Mankato, Minnesota : Capstone Press, 2017. |
Series: You choose books. Ancient Greek myths | Includes bibliographical
references and index. Identifiers: LCCN 2016039231
ISBN 9781515748236 (library binding) | ISBN 9781515748281 (pbk.)
Subjects: LCSH: Hades (Greek deity)—Juvenile literature.
Classification: LCC BL820.P58 H64 2017 | DDC 292.1/3—dc23
LC record available at https://lccn.loc.gov/2016039231

Editorial Credits
Mandy Robbins, editor; Ted Williams, designer;
Kelly Garvin, media researcher; Katy LaVigne, production specialist

IIllustrations by Nadine Takvorian

Image Credits
Alamy/Ivy Close Images, 102

Artistic elements: Shutterstock: Alex Novikov, Eky Studio, reyhan, Samira
Dragonfly, Tymonko Galyna

Printed and bound in Canada.
010050S17

Table of Contents

About Your Adventure

YOU are living in the mythical world of ancient Greece. The bad news is that you must venture into the land of the dead — a place from which the living rarely escape. The good news is that you get to choose what form you will take on your journey. Will you be a Greek hero, or will you take the form of a god? What choice will give you the best odds of survival?

Chapter One sets the scene. Then you choose which path to take. Follow the directions at the bottom of each page. The choices you make determine what happens next. After you finish your path, go back and read the others for more adventures.

YOU CHOOSE the path you take through this mythical adventure.

Hades and the Underworld

According to Greek myth, mighty giants called Titans once ruled the world. Their leader was Cronus. He and his wife, Rhea, had six children called Olympians. Zeus was their leader. His brothers were Hades and Poseidon. Hera, Demeter, and Hestia were their sisters.

After a long, fierce war, the Olympians took control from the Titans. Zeus and his brothers drew lots to divide up their rule. Zeus picked first. He chose the sky as his domain. Poseidon then picked the oceans and the seas. Hades was left with the Underworld, the land of the dead.

Turn the page.

The other Olympians lived on Mount Olympus. But Hades retreated to his underground domain. Hades ruled over the spirits of the dead, but he did not cause death. The god Thanatos did that. Thanatos ended peoples' suffering and helped them move peacefully from one life to the next.

The Underworld was said to be a place hidden deep beneath the ground. Five magical rivers ran through it. The River Styx separated the Underworld from the land of the living.

After people died, the god Hermes led their spirits to the banks of the River Styx near the entrance to the Underworld. Once the spirits entered Hades's kingdom, they went before three judges. The judges were past kings and sons of Zeus. They passed judgments on the dead.

Turn the page.

If someone had been a brave hero or a just ruler, the judges sent him or her to the Elysian Fields. This was a paradise of endless celebrations and feasts. For those deemed wicked, there were the Fields of Punishment. Their spirits faced endless torture. Most spirits were sent to the Asphodel Meadows. This peaceful place was for those who had not achieved any great good nor committed any great evil.

Then there was Tartarus, deep within the Earth. The most evil and dangerous creatures were imprisoned in this dungeon. Zeus sent many of the Titans to Tartarus as punishment.

Gods such as Thanatos and Hecate, the goddess of magic, also lived in the Underworld. Creatures called Furies made the Underworld their home as well. They took revenge on anyone who broke a promise or killed a family member.

There were also many Daemons, or spirits, roaming about. The Arai were the spirits of curses that murder victims placed on their killers. The Empousai were beautiful vampire-like spirits.

From time to time, gods and mortals ventured into the Underworld. Perhaps they wanted to find a loved one who had died. Or maybe they needed advice from the spirit of a wise person. Other times, heroes went on quests to the Underworld.

Hades did not want anyone trespassing in his domain. He played cruel tricks on those from the living world who dared enter his realm uninvited.

Now it's your turn to go on a daring adventure into the Underworld. Will you be a powerful god or a brave mortal as you journey to Hades's realm?

To be a powerful god, turn to page 13.

To be the musician Orpheus, turn to page 33.

To be the hero Theseus or Hercules, turn to page 61.

CHAPTER 2

Persephone and Demeter

Demeter was the goddess of the harvest. She made crops grow. Demeter and Zeus had a daughter named Persephone. Demeter adored her more than anything in the world.

As a young woman, Persephone loved to roam the meadows picking flowers with her friends. One day, an unusual white bloom caught her eye. She wandered away from her group to pick the lovely flower and suddenly disappeared.

That is how the myth of Demeter and Persephone begins. Which goddess will you be?

To be Persephone, turn to page 14.

To be Demeter, turn to page 15.

In the brief moment that you are away from your friends, the ground opens up at your feet. A large, dark figure appears before you. You are shocked to see Hades standing in front of you.

"Zeus has given me permission to marry you," he says. "So I have come to ask for your hand."

You are afraid of Hades, but his offer does have some appeal. Demeter is very protective of you. If you are not in the company of your friends, you must always be by her side. But you are now grown and a powerful goddess yourself. As queen of the Underworld, you would miss the sunny world around you, but marrying Hades would give you freedom from your mother.

Hades hands you a white asphodel flower and asks, "Will you be my queen?"

To say yes to Hades, turn to page 17.✗

To say no to Hades, turn to page 19.

Persephone's friends quickly alert you that she is missing. You race down the hill where they last saw your daughter. The only sign that she was ever there are the flowers she had been collecting.

Your daughter is a goddess. No ordinary mortal or monster could take her in broad daylight. You look at the sky, which gives you an idea.

You rise up toward the sun. As you get closer, you can see that the ball of light is really Helios's golden chariot. It is pulled across the sky by four fiery horses. Helios is god of the sun and the watcher over the land.

"Helios!" you cry, "What happened to my daughter Persephone?"

He is hesitant to answer, but you press him. "She has gone missing. I must know if she is safe."

Turn the page.

"She is as safe as anyone can be in the Underworld," Helios answers.

"Hades took her?" you ask.

"I heard Zeus give Hades permission to marry her," Helios says. "That is why he has taken your daughter away."

With that news, you head for Mount Olympus. You see Zeus sitting on his throne, and you storm over to him.

To attack Zeus, turn to page 21.✕

To curse Zeus, turn to page 22.

You take the flower and say yes. You are not completely sure why. You love nature, and little grows in Hades's dingy realm. But being queen of the Underworld would give you freedom from your mother, which you hadn't realized you craved so badly until now.

Hades offers you his hand, and you take it. Then the opening above you closes. You are plunged into darkness.

In the Underworld, you go from being a goddess of nature to a goddess of vengeance. You command spirits called Arai, who rule over curses and broken promises. But after some time has passed, you begin to miss your mother, which you confess to Hades.

"You are my wife, not my prisoner," he says.

"Then I will go visit my mother," you reply.

Turn the page.

Above ground, you are shocked at how the world has changed. The land is covered in ice and snow. No plants grow anywhere. You visit Zeus and ask him where your mother is.

"When you went missing, she left," he says. "Nothing has grown since."

You return to Hades and tell him the sad news. But he just smiles.

"Once all are dead in the world above, our realm will grow," he says smugly.

You are conflicted. Your heart breaks for the desolate world above. But it does mean your power will grow. Perhaps marrying Hades wasn't the right choice, but you can't change it now.

THE END

To follow another path, turn to page 11.

To learn more about the Underworld, turn to page 103.

You adore nature. You don't want to live in the Underworld where hardly anything grows. You refuse Hades's offer.

"I only asked to be polite," he says. "If you won't come willingly, I will take you."

You turn to call for help, but a hand covers your mouth. Hades drags you down into the Underworld. The opening above you closes. The sun disappears. You are in complete darkness.

"Where are we?" you ask, looking around. Everything is dark and gloomy.

"We are home," Hades says, "in my palace."

"This will never be my home!" you shout.

You storm off, wandering the palace halls. No matter which hallway you turn down, you never find an exit. You are trapped.

Turn the page.

You are unsure how much time has passed. It is hard to tell time when you cannot see the sun. When you see Hades again, you are hungry.

"I hope you are well, my queen," Hades says.

You glare in response, and your stomach grumbles loudly.

"I brought you some food," Hades says.

He sets a tray of food down on a table. It is filled with your favorite fruits and vegetables.

"Please join me," Hades says, gesturing to a bench at the table.

To eat with Hades, turn to page 24.

To go hungry, turn to page 26.

"How dare you let Hades steal her!" you shout.

Furious, you point at the ground beneath his feet. Strangling vines burst through the stone floor. They snake their way up Zeus's legs. Zeus stands, angrily holding his thunderbolt. A flash of light blinds you. You suddenly fly backward.

"Enough!" Zeus shouts. "Allow Hades to have Persephone, or I will cast you into Tartarus."

You had wanted Zeus to bring your daughter back. Now he is threatening you with the worst fate possible. You would go mad in Tartarus.

You have no choice but to accept that your beloved Persephone is now queen of the Underworld. You may never see her again.

THE END

To follow another path, turn to page 11.

To learn more about the Underworld, turn to page 103.

"Hades stole our daughter!" you shout.

"He did not," Zeus replies. "He asked permission to marry Persephone, and I granted it."

"Well I didn't give him permission!" you yell.

"But I did," Zeus says. "The matter is done."

Anger bubbles inside you. You know you could never force Zeus to bring your daughter back. But there are other ways to get what you want.

"The matter is not done," you say. "Until you right this wrong, no flowers will bloom and no crops will grow."

You leave Mount Olympus and hide in the city of Eleusis. Throughout the world grasses die, and trees lose their leaves. The world turns cold and lifeless. Farmers' crops fail to grow. People worry that they will starve. But you don't care. Nothing matters to you except getting your daughter back.

Then one day, you hear from Hermes, messenger of the gods. He tells you that Zeus has ordered Hades to release Persephone from the Underworld. Your plan has worked!

You immediately return to Mount Olympus, where Persephone is waiting for you. Joyfully, you wrap your arms around your daughter.

"My girl! How I've missed you," you exclaim.

"I missed you too!" she cries.

Then Hades appears.

"Enjoy your little reunion," he says. "But she is still my queen."

To hear Hades out, turn to page 25.

To flee with Persephone, turn to page 31.

You see no harm in eating with Hades.
You sit down on the bench.

Instantly, your thoughts grow fuzzy.

"Why I am here?" you ask, turning to the
figure next to you. "And you are . . . who are you?"

Hades laughs. He has tricked you into
sitting on his Chair of Forgetfulness. It robs
you of all your memories. You forget about your
mother and how you got here. You forget how to
speak and how to stand. You are trapped.

Hades moves the chair, with you still on it, to
his throne room. You sit by his side until the end
of time. Stuck on the Chair of Forgetfulness, you
become the silent queen of the Underworld.

THE END

To follow another path, turn to page 11.

To learn more about the Underworld, turn to page 103.

"She ate food of the Underworld," Hades says. "She is mine now."

"Just three pomegranate seeds," Persephone argues. "I was so very hungry."

"That is all it takes," Hades says.

"If you let him take her again," you warn Zeus, "no plant on Earth will ever grow again."

"Then we must compromise," Zeus declares. "She ate three seeds, so Persephone must spend three months of every year with Hades."

The nine months of the year that you spend with Persephone are joyous. The three months she is away, you are incredibly sad. During that time, nothing grows. That time of year is called winter.

THE END

To follow another path, turn to page 11.

To learn more about the Underworld, turn to page 103.

The food Hades brought looks delicious, but you don't trust him. It may be part of a plan to keep you here. You refuse his offer.

Every day, Hades brings you a new offering of food, and he tries to see to your every need. Every day, you refuse him. As a goddess, you can go a long time without eating, even though you're quite hungry and getting weak. You're also starting to feel sorry for Hades. He seems lonely.

You don't remember when you've last eaten, but, finally, you can take it no longer. The next time Hades sets down a tray of food, you sneak three pomegranate seeds. You don't think he will notice. Being a goddess, you don't need to eat much. You hope these tiny morsels will give you strength for now.

Turn the page.

Weeks turn into months. You begin to wonder if you will ever see the sun again. Then one day, Hermes, the messenger of the gods, arrives. He stands before Hades's throne and states, "Zeus demands you release Persephone."

"Then take her," Hades agrees with a sly smile.

Hermes takes you up above ground. You can hardly believe what you see. It is a lifeless world covered in ice and snow.

"Your mother has let nothing grow since you disappeared," Hermes says. "That is why Zeus demanded Hades free you. People are starving."

Hermes takes you to Mount Olympus. There you rejoin your mother. She wraps you in her arms. A moment later, Hades appears.

"What are you doing here?" Demeter asks with a scowl. There is a fiery hate in her eyes.

"I have released Persephone to see her mother," he says. "But she must return to the Underworld."

Your mother looks concerned as she asks you, "Did you eat anything while in the Underworld?"

"Only three pomegranate seeds," you answer.

Hades sneers, "Anyone who eats food of the Underworld belongs to the Underworld."

Demeter turns to Zeus. "If you let him take Persephone back, the world will be barren. Everything will die. You will rule over a wasteland."

"A compromise must be reached," Zeus decides. "Since she ate food of the Underworld, Persephone is part of the Underworld." Then turning to Hades he says, "She ate three seeds, so she will stay with you for three months of the year. The rest of the time she will be with her mother."

Turn the page.

You are satisfied with the arrangement, for the most part. You spend nine months of the year with your mother. Those are happy times, when the meadows are filled with flowers. Then for three months, you join Hades to rule the Underworld while the world above is cold and barren. You grow to accept your role as queen of the dead.

THE END

To follow another path, turn to page 11.

To learn more about the Underworld, turn to page 103.

You worry that Hades will take Persephone back to the Underworld. You won't let that happen. You grab your daughter and flee.

But no matter where you go, Helios tracks you down. Zeus is furious at your defiance.

"Enough!" he says. "If you will not make the crops grow, then I will send both you and Persephone to the Underworld to serve Hades."

You are now a permanent resident of the Underworld. While Persephone is Hades's queen, you care for his gardens. They are full of poisonous and toxic plants. You spend your days tending these deadly plants instead of enjoying the sunny world above.

THE END

To follow another path, turn to page 11.

To learn more about the Underworld, turn to page 103.

CHAPTER 3

Orpheus

Mnemosyne was one of the Titans who did not fight against the Olympians. She and Zeus had nine daughters called Muses.

Zeus's son Apollo helped raise the Muses. He was the god of light, and also the god of music, medicine, and science. Each muse became a patron of an art form.

You are Orpheus, son of Calliope. She is the muse of epic poetry. Your father is King Oeagrus, ruler of the city of Thrace. Your older brother Linus is a marvelous musician. He teaches you to play the lyre. Your talent becomes so great that, one day, you play for the god Apollo.

Turn the page.

Apollo is impressed with your talent. He gives you his own lyre as a gift. Inspired, you study music and poetry even more. Those who hear you play say your songs cause trees to sway and rivers to change course.

You become a renowned musician. Word of your skill reaches the ears of the great hero Jason. His father once ruled the city of Iolcus. To take back his father's lost throne, Jason must find the magical Golden Fleece. For this quest, he calls upon heroes from across the land. These men are called the Argonauts because they sail on a ship called the *Argos*. You are surprised when Jason asks you to be one of them.

In the quest for the Golden Fleece, you leave the fighting to the heroes. Your role is to encourage the Argonauts. Your music uplifts their spirits and gives them strength.

Then one day, you get the chance to be a real hero. The Argonauts are on their way home after finding the Golden Fleece. Suddenly the men become entranced by beautiful voices singing. It is coming from an outcropping of rocks up ahead. The voices sing:

Come brave sailor, so strong and bold.
Come brave sailor, be our hero.

You seem to be the only man unaffected by the eerie music. As the ship nears the rock, you realize the danger. Three beautiful women sit on the outcropping. They sing and motion for the men to come to them.

"Sirens," you whisper under your breath. You've heard of them. They lure men to their deaths with song. You have to do something or Jason and the Argonauts will be doomed.

Turn the page.

Suddenly, you have an idea. You sing as you strum your lyre:

Listen to me, my brave Argonauts.
We have found what we have sought.
Now our home calls to us.
We must return to Iolcus.

As your voice grows in volume, it drowns out the sirens. You see the men look at you, confused. Some are on the verge of leaping into the water. Others are fighting for a look at the sirens. But your music sways them. You sing:

Now our home calls us.
We must return to Iolcus.
So grab your oars and row.
Row until the west winds blow.

The men sit back down and take up their oars. Jason returns to his place at the rudder.

Turn the page.

You continue your song until the sirens are out of earshot. Your idea to break the sirens' spell worked! You saved the day with your music and have proven yourself a true hero.

After a long journey, the *Argos* finally reaches Iolcus. Jason regains his throne. Eventually you return home and continue to play music.

People and animals alike are enchanted by your songs. One day when you are playing in the woods, you spy a shy wood nymph peeking around a tree. Her name is Eurydice. Your music has drawn her out of her hiding spot. You continue to play songs for her, and the two of you eventually fall in love.

Soon you marry. You have a lovely wedding filled with music, laughter, and poetry. But what starts out as a happy day does not end well.

Aristaeus, a son of Apollo, also loves Eurydice. When no one is watching, he tries to steal her away, but Eurydice runs from him. During the chase, she steps on a venomous snake that bites her in the ankle.

You hear her scream and rush to her side. But there is nothing you can do. The snake's venom has quickly worked its way through her body. Not even the god Apollo can save her life.

She dies in your arms, and you are left grief-stricken. You've just lost the love of your life. In your sadness, you make an impossible vow.

"I will go to the Underworld," you claim, "and bring Eurydice back!"

"Hades will never release her spirit," your mother says.

Turn the page.

But you are determined. You learn of the Taenarian gate, a secret entrance to the Underworld. It is tucked under an outcropping of rocks. You step into the dark cave. The chill in the air makes you shudder.

After a long walk down into darkness, the cave opens up into a world of shadows. Before you is the River Styx. Misty spirits walk along its shore. They slowly drift toward the skeletal figure of Charon in his boat. He ferries the spirits of the dead to the Underworld. On the other side of the river, you see the gates to the Underworld.

As each spirit approaches Charon holds out his hand. The spirits drop coins into Charon's palm and board his boat.

Once the ferry is full, Charon uses a long pole to push his boat away from the shore. He carries the spirits to the other side of the river.

Eventually, it is your turn. Charon holds out his hand for payment.

To pay Charon with a coin, turn to page 42.

To pay Charon with a song, turn to page 43.

You place a coin in Charon's palm, but he doesn't let you on the ferry. Slowly, spirits of the dead gather behind you. They are getting restless. You are in their way.

"I must get to the other side!" you shout.

Charon merely points back toward the way you've come. The crowd of spirits grows larger and angrier. They push you past the water's edge.

You plunge into the River Styx, and its dark waters swallow you. Hands from below pull you deep beneath the surface and drown you.

Then you climb back on shore. You approach Charon again, and this time he steps aside for you. You are now one of the spirits of the dead.

THE END

To follow another path, turn to page 11.

To learn more about the Underworld, turn to page 103.

Charon demands a toll from anyone wishing to cross the River Styx. You know he will only transport spirits of the dead. Since you are still one of the living, you guess that he will not accept a coin as payment from you. You need to find another way to convince him to take you across.

Music has always been your most powerful gift. So when Charon holds out his skeletal hand, you do not give him a coin. You pull out your lyre and begin to play.

You decide a funeral song would be the most respectful kind of music to play here. You strum your lyre, playing soft, quiet notes. The gathering of spirits behind you calms down. They stop their shuffling and mumbling and simply listen. Charon bows his head. After a few moments, he lowers his hand and steps aside for you.

Turn the page.

You play on as Charon takes you across the river. You worry he may change his mind otherwise.

He sets you on the opposite shore. You don't know where to go, so you follow the spirits drifting from the riverbank. They lead you to a towering stone wall. It stretches as far as you can see.

The spirits of the dead pour through an open gate in the wall. But a massive three-headed dog blocks your way. This beast is Cerberus. He guards the gates to the Underworld. Cerberus only allows spirits of the dead to enter.

You are no warrior, so you doubt you could beat Cerberus in a fight. But if your music can sway Charon, perhaps it will have an effect on Cerberus.

You begin to strum your lyre. Instead of playing a funeral song, you play a lullaby. Cerberus stops growling and tilts his heads to listen.

You keep playing, gently plucking the strings and humming along. Cerberus sits and then lies down in front of you. He rests his heads on his front paws. His eyes slowly close. You don't take a step forward until the beast's heavy breathing turns into snores.

Once inside the gate, you watch the spirits drift toward a large dome. That is where the three judges will decide their fates. But you do not need to see them to know where to go. You are sure your wife will be in the Asphodel Meadows, where most spirits end up.

Just past the dome, there is a path that leads through the meadow. You begin to walk down it. In the other direction you can see Hades's palace.

To search for Eurydice in the Asphodel Meadows, turn to page 46.

To ask Hades to release Eurydice, turn to page 48.

Hades is not a kind, forgiving god. He won't
take kindly to you trespassing in his realm.
He doesn't let the dead leave his kingdom,
and you doubt he would let the living leave
either. You decide to search for Eurydice yourself.
You step off the path and are swarmed by spirits.

"Eurydice, my love!" you cry. There is no reply.

You walk on, calling your wife's name.
Everything around you is gray. It's hard to tell one
landmark from the next.

Every way you turn, spirits block your path.
You quickly lose your way. The only thing you can
think to do is play a song.

Oh Eurydice, my lovely wife,
I've come to take you away from here.
Oh Eurydice, love of my life,
I've come to take you away, my dear.

"Orpheus?" you hear.

"Eurydice!" you call out.

Suddenly, you notice the spirits of the dead have surrounded you. Again and again, they echo your name, "Orpheus! Orpheus! Orpheus!"

They are restless and beg, "Play for us! Play for us! Play for us!"

And that is your fate, and your punishment for sneaking into the Underworld. You are forever stuck in the Asphodel Meadows surrounded by spirits begging you to play. You play until your fingers bleed, your arms grow numb, and you forget why you came to the Underworld in the first place.

THE END

To follow another path, turn to page 11.

To learn more about the Underworld, turn to page 103.

Instead of searching the Asphodel Meadows for Eurydice, you go straight to Hades's palace. You will ask the god directly to release your wife from the Underworld.

You know that Hades does not like intruders coming into his realm. That is why he has Charon and Cerberus to keep out the living. While you fear confronting him, you have dealt with other gods, such as Apollo. You know it is better to ask for something directly than to try to be sneaky. To do so and be caught would mean a horrific punishment.

You pass through the Fields of Punishment and see King Ixion. He had tried to steal the goddess Hera away from her husband Zeus. For his punishment, he has been strapped to a flaming wheel that spins around and around. You play a soothing song to ease his pain.

Then you see King Tantalus. Among his many crimes, he had tried to steal ambrosia, which is the food of the gods. As punishment, he stands in a pool of water beneath a fruit tree. He is constantly hungry and thirsty. Anytime he reaches for fruit, the branches rise up out of his grasp. Anytime he reaches for water, it flows away from him. You play a song of feasts and parties that you hope will help quench his thirst and hunger.

Next, you see King Sisyphus. He made the unpardonable mistake of telling some of Zeus's secrets. His punishment is to forever push a large rock up a hill. Once he reaches the top, the boulder rolls back down, and he has to start all over again. For him, you play a quiet, soothing song, to help his aching muscles.

Turn the page.

Finally, you reach Hades's palace. Whenever anything, monster or spirit, stands in your way, you strum your lyre. The magic of your music makes them leave you alone. You walk through the palace to Hades's throne room. He glares down at you. His wife, Persephone, is at his side.

"I have heard your songs echoing throughout my realm," Hades says thoughtfully, with perhaps a touch of anger. "Why are you here?"

So far it is music that has gotten you through every situation. You could play a song to soothe Hades's anger. Or you could play a song to tell the Queen of the Underworld, Persephone, the sadness you felt, losing your wife.

To play a song for Persephone, turn to page 52.
To play a song for Hades, turn to page 55.

Your songs have swayed men and monsters. But you doubt they would have an effect on the powerful god Hades. So you turn your attention to the goddess Persephone.

The Queen of the Underworld is a goddess of nature and growing things. She has to spend a few months of the year in the gloomy Underworld because of a trick Hades played on her. The rest of the year, she can enjoy the sun and the rain.

For her, you play a song of sadness. A song of longing for the things you love. You sing of losing your wife and the loss you feel for her now that she is in the Underworld.

By the end of your song, Persephone is in tears. She leans over to Hades and says, "He deserves a reward for such a lovely song."

Hades scowls at you. Then he turns to his wife, and asks, "What is a worthy payment for one so gifted in words?"

"Give him back his wife," Persephone says.

"Very well," Hades grumbles. "Leave my realm and I will do as my wife asks. Your Eurydice will follow you out of the Underworld, but if you look back or speak to her before you both are in the sunlight, she will be trapped here. Now go."

You quickly turn and rush out of the throne room. You do as Hades says. You exit his palace and follow the path back to the gates to the Underworld. Cerberus does not stop you from leaving. Charon is waiting to carry you back across the river. You rush over to the tunnel that leads back to the world of the living.

Turn the page.

Not once do you look back. But you hurry, as the sooner you step into the sunlight, the sooner you will see your wife again.

As you walk through the cave, doubt starts to creep into your thoughts. You know that Hades is a trickster. You've seen how he has punished Tantalus and Sisyphus. Still, you do not look back. You listen. You hope to hear Eurydice's footsteps behind you or hear her breathe. But you hear nothing — not a sound. There is no hint that she is behind you.

Finally, you are at the entrance to the cave. You step out into the sunlight. It warms your skin.

To keep walking, turn to page 57.

To look back, turn to page 58.

So far, your music has gotten you through almost every situation in your life. It inspired the god Apollo to give you a lyre. It helped you save the Argonauts from the sirens. It won Eurydice's heart. So you play a song for Hades.

Hades is a god of all the riches that the Earth holds. So you play a joyous song of endless wealth. The god smiles and laughs as you play.

When you are done, he applauds. Persephone remains quiet, staring at you scornfully.

"Well done, master musician. Well done," Hades says. "And I have just the reward for someone such as yourself."

"You will release my wife?" you ask.

"No, no," the god says. "You will entertain those in the Fields of Punishment."

Turn the page.

Then you are whisked away by several shadowy spirits. You find yourself chained to a rock in the middle of the Fields of Punishment. Screams and wails of tortured spirits fill the air.

You strum your lyre, hoping to ease the pain of those suffering around you. But it's not music that comes from your lyre when you pluck its strings. Instead, you hear a deafening screech. No matter what notes you attempt to play, the sound that comes out is ear-shattering noise. And from this day throughout eternity, you are forced to play and listen to this horrible sound.

THE END

To follow another path, turn to page 11.

To learn more about the Underworld, turn to page 103.

Though you are in the sunlight, you do not look back. Eurydice may not have exited the cave yet. You walk a little farther, so that Eurydice can step into the sunlight. But a dark cloud follows you out of the cave. It casts a shadow that the sunlight cannot penetrate. The cloud keeps Eurydice from standing in the sunlight, and if you ever look back at her, she will be taken back to the Underworld.

You fall to your knees and cry. Hades has tricked you! He has let your wife leave the Underworld but kept you from ever seeing her again.

You live the rest of your life in sadness. You know your wife is close, but you cannot see or speak to her. You are too heartbroken to even play the music that she once loved.

THE END

To follow another path, turn to page 11.

To learn more about the Underworld, turn to page 103.

You step into the sunlight and look back. To your horror, Eurydice has not exited the cave. She is not standing in the sunlight. For an instant, you see her shadowy figure in the tunnel.

"Orpheus," you hear her whisper.

Then black tendrils wrap themselves around Eurydice. You race over to her. But she is pulled back into the cave before you can reach her.

"Orpheus!" she screams.

And that is the last you see of your wife.

Not long after this, your life ends as well. To honor you, the Muses take your lyre and place it up in the stars as a constellation so that you will always be remembered.

THE END

To follow another path, turn to page 11.

To learn more about the Underworld, turn to page 103.

CHAPTER 4

Theseus and Hercules

In ancient Greek lore, heroes sometimes ventured into the Underworld to gain important knowledge. Other times, they braved the Underworld on a quest to get something from Hades's realm. That is true of the Greek heroes Theseus and Hercules.

Theseus was famous for slaying the Minotaur. This half-man, half bull beast had lived in an endless maze known as the Labyrinth. Hercules was famous for accomplishing nearly impossible tasks called labors. He killed the fearsome Nemean Lion and captured the monstrous Cretan Bull.

Turn the page.

Theseus once journeyed with Hercules. Hercules was on a quest to retrieve Hippolyte's belt. She was queen of the Amazons, a tribe of warrior women. Her belt was a gift from Ares, god of war. It made her the best fighter among the Amazons. After retrieving the belt, Hercules and Theseus parted.

"Do you think perhaps we'll see each other again?" Hercules asked.

"Let us hope. Until then, safe travels, my friend," Theseus replied.

Little did these brave heroes know that their paths would cross in the Underworld. For both ended up on quests that eventually led them there.

To be Hercules, turn to page 63.

To be Theseus, turn to page 68.

You are the mighty hero Hercules. Your mother is Princess Alcmene, and your father is Zeus, the ruler of the gods. With such a powerful father, it is no surprise that you have grown into the strongest man alive. You've also become famous for your many brave deeds.

While Zeus supports you, his wife, Hera, does not. She hates you and all the other children Zeus has fathered by mortal women. One day, she causes you to go insane. In your madness, you accidentally kill your wife and children. When you come to your senses, you are horrified and guilt-ridden by their deaths at your hand.

Not knowing what to do, you seek out the Oracle of Delphi for advice. The prophet tells you that you can gain the gods' forgiveness for your horrible acts. But you must first perform 10 tasks for King Eurystheus of Tiryns.

Turn the page.

Eurystheus gives you tasks that he hopes you will fail at. He orders you to slay the many-headed Hydra. With the help of your nephew, Iolaus, you manage to defeat this monster. The king also commands you to clean out the Augean stables, which have filled up with 30 years' worth of horse manure. You accomplish this feat by diverting a river to run through the stables.

You successfully complete nine of the tasks the king has asked of you. You are now about to finish your 10th and final labor. Eurystheus had asked you to retrieve Geryon's cattle. Geryon was a three-headed giant with six legs. You fought and killed him. Now you lead Geryon's herd into Eurystheus's palace.

"I have done as you have asked," you tell the king. "I have earned the gods' forgiveness."

"No," King Eurystheus says. "You were to do 10 labors for me, but you cheated."

"How so?" you exclaim.

"Your nephew helped you defeat the Hydra," the king says. "And you used a river to clean out the Augean stables."

"But the tasks were completed," you say.

"But they were not done by your hand alone," he replies. "I demand two more labors."

You're afraid of what tasks the king may think up next. Several times already you've nearly been killed on your quests. You are exhausted. You do not wish to risk your life for the whims of the king any longer. But you also worry that the gods will not forgive you if you do not do as Eurystheus asks.

Turn the page.

The oracle said you had to complete the tasks that King Eurystheus set out for you. If he says two tasks were not done right, then you must complete two more tasks. You are determined to earn the gods' forgiveness for killing your family.

"What is my next task?" you ask the king.

"Bring me the apples of the Hesperides," he says.

The Hesperides are woodland nymphs. They care for a tree that grows golden apples. The tree is guarded by a 100-headed dragon. Amazingly, you are able to complete this task. But it is not nearly as difficult as the last task the king asks of you.

"Fetch Cerberus for me," he says with a laugh.

Cerberus is a giant three-headed dog. Worse yet, he guards the gates to the Underworld. You have to venture into the land of the dead, defeat Cerberus, and somehow return with the monster.

The task seems impossible, even to you. And you don't even know how to reach the Underworld. Only the dead are allowed to go there.

You need a god's help. But being a hero means you have had to challenge the gods to protect people. You've wrestled Ares, the god of war, and battled Apollo, the god of light. Not many of the gods support you, especially after you killed your family. Two gods that are not angry with you are your father, Zeus, and Demeter, goddess of the harvest.

Which one do you call on for help?

To seek Zeus's help, turn to page 79.

To seek Demeter's help, turn to page 81.

You are the Greek hero Theseus. Your mother is Princess Aethra of Troezen. Growing up, you did not know who your father was. Your mother kept his identity secret until you reached adulthood.

"I had to protect you from his enemies," she says. "But I can tell you now. Your father is King Aegeus."

"The ruler of Athens?" you ask, shocked.

Your mother explains that years ago Athens lost a war to the kingdom of Crete. Crete's King Minos demanded a horrible price from your father. Every nine years, Athens must send seven young men and seven young women to Crete as tributes. They are sent into the Labyrinth, a maze where the Minotaur lives. This half-man, half-bull beast eats the tributes.

You travel to Athens to find your father. On the way, you battle bandits and defeat giants. Your father is impressed with your deeds and welcomes you as heir to his throne. You then go on a quest to slay the Minotaur and succeed. Stories of your deeds spread throughout Greece. When your father dies, you become king of Athens.

During your time as ruler, you journey with the mighty Hercules to battle the Amazons, and you defend the city from invaders. You gain fame as a mighty hero and a wise king.

Then one day, years later, a herd of your prized cattle goes missing. You take a couple of your guards and go investigate. You eventually find your missing herd grazing in a field. But there is only one bandit. He is waiting for you at the edge of the field.

Turn the page.

"How dare you steal from me?" you say to the man.

"You must be Theseus," he says, smiling. "I am Pirithous of Thessaly, and I wish to challenge you to combat."

It surprises you that this man is so daring. You are king of a powerful city. You have soldiers who are tasked with arresting common criminals, such as cattle thieves.

To accept Pirithous's challenge, turn to page 72.

To deny Pirithous's challenge, turn to page 77.

"Is that why you stole my cattle?" you ask.
"To challenge me?"

"I wanted to find out if you are truly as heroic
as rumors say you are," Pirithous replies.

"Then draw your sword," you say.

He draws his weapon and rushes you.
You are quick to draw your sword and easily
block his blow.

You battle back and forth. The clangs of
your swords ring out. But neither of you can take
the advantage. He attacks, and you knock his
sword aside. You lunge, and he blocks your blows.
The battle rages until you are both exhausted.

"I am impressed," Pirithous gasps. "I never
thought you would be this good."

"Shall we call a truce then?" you ask.

Pirithous offers you his hand. "Truce," he says.

You and Pirithous become the best of friends. After one of your many adventures, Pirithous comes to you with an interesting idea.

"Brave heroes such as us should marry daughters of Zeus," he says. Zeus's daughters are powerful women and goddesses.

"Surely you don't mean Athena or Artemis?" you ask. Athena is the goddess of wisdom and nearly as powerful as Zeus. Artemis is the goddess of the hunt and deadly with her bow.

"No, no, but there is Helen of Sparta," he suggests.

"She is the most beautiful woman in the world," you add.

"Then you should marry her," he says.

Turn the page.

"And who shall you marry?" you ask.

"I wish to marry Persephone," your friend says with a cocky smile.

Persephone is the daughter of Zeus and the goddess Demeter. She is a goddess of nature. She is also married to Hades, ruler of the Underworld.

You fear Pirithous's plan is too daring. But after he helps you capture Helen, you have no choice but to help him win Persephone. During the warm months, the young goddess stays with her mother up on Mount Olympus.

"There is no way we could reach her up there," you tell your friend.

"But it is winter," Pirithous says. "She is not up on Mount Olympus during this time of year."

"No, she is in the Underworld," you whisper.

"Then that is where we will go," he replies.

"But how?" you ask. "Only the dead know the way to the Underworld."

"Have you heard of Orpheus, the famed musician?" Pirithous asks. You nod. He was one of the men called Argonauts who traveled with Jason on a quest to find the magical Golden Fleece.

"After the death of his wife, Eurydice, he went to the Underworld to get her back," Pirithous explains. "He entered through a secret entrance, and I know where it is."

You and Pirithous travel across Greece. He leads you to a strange rock outcropping that hides a dark cave. A cold breeze comes from the opening, and the smell of rot fills the air.

Turn the page.

You follow Pirithous into the dark tunnel. Your path leads to the River Styx. On its banks are hundreds of spirits of the dead. They stand before a tall, skeletal figure dressed in dark robes. In the water next to him is a wooden ferryboat.

"That is Charon, the ferryman," Pirithous whispers. "For a coin, he carries the spirits of the dead across the river."

As you approach, Charon holds out his hand to you.

To give Charon a coin, turn to page 85.

To force your way onto Charon's boat, turn to page 87.

"How dare a common thief challenge me," you say. To your guards, you shout, "Kill him!"

Your guards lower their spears, but Pirithous does not look worried.

"I am no common thief," he says. "I am the king of Lapiths."

Then you watch in amazement as Pirithous quickly dispatches your guards without even drawing his sword.

"I stole your cattle only to get your attention," he says. "I wanted to see if you were really as heroic as I'd heard."

While your guards lay on the ground groaning in pain, Pirithous struts up to you. "But now I know better," he says.

Pirithous turns and walks away.

Turn the page.

You think the matter is done and that you will never hear from him again. But he tells people of your encounter. The story quickly spreads across Greece. It ruins your reputation, and other rulers no longer fear you. They join together and march an army to Athens. You lose your kingdom and are sent into exile, never to return.

THE END

To follow another path, turn to page 11.

To learn more about the Underworld, turn to page 103.

You father is ruler of the Olympians. You hope he is willing to help you. You journey to the bottom of Mount Olympus and look up at its peak.

"Father, Zeus, I need your help!" you shout.

You have never asked for his help before, not even when battling gods or fighting monsters. You hope he will come to your aid just this once. Suddenly a blur of motion comes whirling down the mountain. It stops right in front of you. It is Hermes, the messenger of the gods.

"Do you have word from Zeus?" you ask.

"I do," he says. From the tone of his voice, you can tell it is not good. "Hera prevents him and any of the other gods from helping you. You must achieve this quest on your own."

Turn the page.

Suddenly, Hermes is gone.

You spend the rest of your life searching for a way to enter the Underworld. It is not until many years later, upon your death, that you find it. But it is too late for you to finish your quest. The three judges then send you to the Fields of Punishment, where you are tortured for eternity for killing your family.

THE END

To follow another path, turn to page 11.

To learn more about the Underworld, turn to page 103.

You know you cannot rely on your father. His wife, Hera, caused you to go mad in the first place. She probably wouldn't let him help you even if he wanted to.

But Demeter is the mother of Persephone, queen of the Underworld. Long ago, Hades kidnapped her daughter. Demeter searched for a way to reach the Underworld and get Persephone back. If anyone can guide you there, she can.

You have heard that there is a temple dedicated to Demeter in the city of Eleusis. You go there to seek help. At the temple, one of the priests tells you of a secret entrance to the Underworld.

"Travel to the city of Taenarum in Laconia," he says. "There you will find a rocky outcropping. Beneath it is a cave that leads into Hades's realm."

Turn the page.

You do as he says and find the outcropping. It hides the secret entrance to the Underworld. The tunnel leads you down to the shores of the River Styx. Around you is a desolate landscape. All is gray and rocky. Hundreds of misty spirits walk toward the bank of the river.

They all stop in front of a skeletal figure in a small ferryboat. It is Charon, the ferryman. He asks for a coin from each spirit of the dead. This is payment for carrying them across the River Styx.

But you are not dead, so you doubt he will willingly carry you across. When you walk up to him, he reaches out his hand. Instead of pulling out a coin, you draw your sword.

"I demand that you carry me across," you say.

Behind you the dead mumble, "It is Hercules! Hercules is here!"

Turn the page.

Charon scowls, but your skill as a warrior must have reached even his ears. He lets you board his ferry and carries you across to the opposite shore. There, a towering wall stretches as far as you can see. Spirits drift through the open gate, but as you approach, you hear a growl. A large three-headed dog blocks your path. It is Cerberus, the goal of your quest. He is held back by a thick chain.

To battle Cerberus, turn to page 90.

To speak with Hades first, turn to page 93.

Pirithous drops a coin into the ferryman's palm. But Charon does not step out of the way. Instead, he points in the direction that you had come from.

"I thought we could just give him a coin," Pirithous says.

You glance around. Misty spirits surround you. Several step up to Charon and give him a coin. He steps aside to let them enter the ferryboat.

Then it dawns on you. You are still alive. Charon only ferries across the spirits of the dead. You explain this to Pirithous, and he curses.

"Then we will swim across," he says boldly.

"No!" you shout as he dives in the dark waters of the Styx.

Turn the page.

As Pirithous starts to swim across the river, ghostly hands reach up from its depths. They pull Pirithous beneath the waves. He tries to fight them off, but there are too many.

A few moments later, a gray spirit walks up to you. It is your friend Pirithous. He is now among the spirits of the dead. He waves goodbye as he boards Charon's ferry.

With your friend dead, you have no reason to continue on your quest. You return home. But there, you find that Helen's family members have come to take her away. They sack the city of Athens and leave your kingdom in ruins.

THE END

To follow another path, turn to page 11.

To learn more about the Underworld, turn to page 103.

Pirithous reaches for a coin, but you stop him.

"Charon will only ferry the dead," you say.

"We could swim," your friend suggests.

But you see something moving beneath the river's dark surface. You do not want to risk facing whatever is in the river.

"How did Orpheus get across?" you ask.

"He persuaded Charon with a song," he says.

You have an idea.

"We may not be master musicians like he was," you explain. "Be we are master swordsmen."

You draw your sword and level it at Charon. Pirithous does the same. The ferryman scowls before letting you step onto his boat. He ferries you to the opposite shore.

Turn the page.

A towering wall stretches to the left and right. But in front of you, there is a gate. The spirits of the dead pass through it.

"Cerberus guards the gate," Pirithous says.

The massive three-headed dog snarls and lurches at you, but he is held back by a thick chain.

"Orpheus lulled Cerberus to sleep with a song," Pirithous says. "Shall we use your trick again?"

Just then, a large crack forms in the wall next to the gate.

"Come," a voice beckons.

Through the opening, you see Hades on his throne. Beside him sits Persephone.

Pirithous steps through, and you follow.

"Charon told me that two trespassers had come into my realm," Hades says. "Why are you here?"

Ever confident, Pirithous walks up to Hades's throne. Instead of talking to him, though, he turns his gaze to Persephone.

"I wish to talk to you," he says with a smile.

"He *is* a daring one," Persephone tells Hades.

"As is he," Hades says, pointing to you. "The bandits and giants that you have slain have spoken of you."

"The dead always make their killers out to be villains," Persephone laughs. "Tell us your side of the story."

"Dine with us," Hades beckons. "Sit down."

Next to the table is a stone bench.

To sit and eat with Hades, turn to page 97.

To insist on talking to Persephone, turn to page 100.

You have struggled for many years to reach this point — the end of your labors. With Cerberus in sight, you can think of nothing but quickly finishing the task.

You charge Cerberus. He howls at you with one of his heads. Another head snaps at you, and you knock it aside. Another lunges at your legs, and you jump over it.

Now you are behind the beast. You grab the chain that holds him and yank on it. Cerberus flips onto his back. You dive at him, swinging your fists at his heads. Every time you connect, a head goes limp. Soon the battle is over.

But your joy is short-lived. Suddenly, the wall rips open. An angry Hades steps through it.

"How dare you enter my realm uninvited!" he shouts.

Turn the page.

He walks over to Cerberus and pats the beast. Cerberus wakens and snarls at you. Hades unhooks his chain.

"Perhaps this will make the fight more fair," snarls Hades.

As you were watching Hades, the spirits of the dead had surrounded you. They grasp at your arms and legs.

When Cerberus pounces, you are unable to move. His teeth sink deep into your shoulder, and he quickly ends your life.

THE END

To follow another path, turn to page 11.

To learn more about the Underworld, turn to page 103.

You know that Hades does not like uninvited guests in his realm. So you worry that if you simply take Cerberus, he will be angry with you.

"Hades!" you shout. "I have come to ask a favor of you."

A moment later, Cerberus steps aside. You walk through the gate, and he does not attack.

From here a path leads to Hades's palace. You walk past the Asphodel Meadows, where spirits of the dead drift about. You walk past the Fields of Punishment, where screams of the tortured fill the air. You enter Hades's palace and find the ruler of the Underworld sitting on his throne with his queen, Persephone, by his side.

"So the son of Zeus has come to visit me on his quest," Hades laughs.

Turn the page.

"Then you know why I am here?" you ask.

"I do. I have heard of the task that King Eurystheus has for you," Hades says. "It is rather bold of him to send someone to my realm."

You listen patiently as the god speaks.

"And because of that, I will allow you to take Cerberus back to him," Hades says. "That is, if you can defeat my guard dog."

You thank Hades for giving you permission to complete your task. As you leave the palace, you see an odd sight. Your friend Theseus and his companion Pirithous are sitting on a bench absolutely still. They stare blankly at the table in front of them.

You walk over to the table and tug on Pirithous. He is bound to the bench by vines. No matter how hard you tug, you cannot free him.

You have better luck with Theseus. With a mighty tug, you free him.

"Hercules!" he cries. "What are you doing here?"

You tell him of your quest. He tells you that he and Pirithous were on a quest to capture Persephone, but Hades tricked them into sitting on the Chair of Forgetfulness. You then lead Theseus back to the gates of the Underworld.

"Let us say goodbye here," you say. "I must complete this task on my own. You should leave the Underworld before Hades knows you've escaped."

"Thank you, my friend," he says.

You distract Cerberus so Theseus can sneak past. Then you duck under the dog's snapping jaws and wrap your muscular arms around its three necks.

Turn the page.

You lift Cerberus up in the air and slam him down on the ground. Cerberus whimpers, and you know you have won the battle.

You take Cerberus back to King Eurystheus in chains. When you enter his throne room, Cerberus barks and snarls, and the scared king hides in a large brass pot.

"I will let him loose," you warn. "If you do not agree that my labors are complete."

"Yes, yes, you are free to go," the king replies.

You return Cerberus to the Underworld, having earned the gods' forgiveness. And because of your heroic deeds, Zeus makes you immortal. You join the gods up on Mount Olympus.

THE END

To follow another path, turn to page 11.

To learn more about the Underworld, turn to page 103.

You see no choice but to sit with Hades and Persephone. Maybe Pirithous can win Persephone's heart with tales of his bravery.

You nod to your friend. Then you both take a seat. Suddenly your mind goes foggy.

"What did you want to talk about?" you ask Hades. He laughs. You turn to your friend to ask why you are there, but you do not recognize the person sitting next to you.

"Who are you?" Pirithous asks.

You realize you have forgotten your name.

"I don't know," you say.

As you sit there in Hades's Chair of Forgetfulness, all of your memories escape you. You forget how to speak and how to stand. You are trapped.

Turn the page.

Years later, strong hands yank you from your seat. All of your memories come rushing back. You look up to see an old friend.

"Hercules!" you shout in surprise.

"Help me with Pirithous," he says as he yanks on your friend's arm.

Even with both of you straining, you are unable to pull Pirithous from the bench. Stony vines have wrapped around him, holding him firmly to his seat.

"It is no use," Hercules says. "And you need to leave before Hades learns that you are free."

"But why are you here?" you ask.

"I am on a quest to capture Cerberus," he says. "This is something I must do alone, but I will lead you to the Underworld's gate."

You follow Hercules to the gate where Cerberus is snapping and growling. The dog leaps at you. But Hercules grabs him as you rush away, back to the land of the living.

It is now that you face the fact that you failed in your quest. Worse yet, you lost a good friend. But at least you survived. You are one of the few mortals to enter the Underworld and return to the land of the living. The tale of your adventure will be told throughout the ages.

THE END

To follow another path, turn to page 11.

To learn more about the Underworld, turn to page 103.

You know that anyone who eats something in the Underworld will be trapped there forever. The offering of a feast is probably a trick. Hades is not fond of trespassers.

You whisper to Pirithous, "I think it's a trick." He nods and turns to Hades.

"Oh kind and gracious ruler of the Underworld," your friend begins. "I thank you for this offer, but we do not wish to bother you. I am only here to speak with Persephone."

Hades laughs. "They are brave," he tells his wife. "And rude."

"At least Orpheus played a song for me," Persephone says.

"Since you won't accept my hospitality, perhaps you can entertain us," Hades says. "Come, my Arai!"

Several dark, whirling shapes breeze into the throne room. They look a bit like women, but with gruesome features.

"Every time you killed a monster or villain, they cursed you," Hades says. "Now it is time for these spirits to avenge their deaths."

The shadowy creatures descend upon you. There is one for every monster and man you have killed. They take revenge by killing you the same way you killed them. You once killed a giant with a club, so one of the Arai attacks you with a club. You killed the Minotaur with a sword, so one of them attacks you with a sword. After each death, you are reborn only to suffer another death.

THE END

To follow another path, turn to page 11.

To learn more about the Underworld, turn to page 103.

CHAPTER 5

More About the Underworld

Each path in this book covers a popular myth about the Underworld. Some of these stories helped ancient Greeks understand the world around them.

The myth of Demeter and Persephone explained the seasons. In the story, Hades kidnapped Persephone to make her his queen. But Demeter caused the world to turn into a wintry wasteland until her daughter was returned. Hades then tricked a hungry Persephone into eating three pomegranate seeds so she would be forced to stay.

Turn the page.

Hades might have kept Persephone with him forever, but Zeus needed Demeter to let the plants grow again, so he struck a bargain. Persephone could return to her mother. But because she ate three pomegranate seeds in the Underworld, she had to stay with Hades for three months each year. During those months, Demeter missed her daughter so much that she would not let plants grow. Ancient Greeks used this myth to explain the changing of seasons.

Orpheus's story is probably the most popular myth about someone willingly venturing into the Underworld. After his wife's death, he vowed to bring her back from the land of the dead. Hades told Orpheus that Eurydice would follow him out of the Underworld. But if he looked back before they were both standing in the sunlight, Eurydice would return to the Underworld, and Orpheus would never see her again.

On the trek out of the Underworld, doubt set in with Orpheus. He did not know if he could trust Hades. And while he waited to look back until he had stepped into the light, it was still too soon. Eurydice was still in the cave. When Orpheus looked back at her, she was dragged back to the Underworld.

The myth of Orpheus and Eurydice explained that death was permanent. No one, no matter how hard they tried, could bring someone back from Hades's realm. The ruler of the Underworld would not allow anyone to escape.

The stories of Theseus's and Hercules's journeys showed that Hades was just and hard to fool. Hercules went on a quest to capture Cerberus as one of his labors. He succeeded because he first asked Hades's permission to take Cerberus.

Turn the page.

Theseus, on the other hand, went to the Underworld on a fool's errand with his friend. He attempted to steal the queen of the Underworld away from Hades. When he entered the Underworld, he was king of one of the most powerful cities in Greece. But because he got trapped on the Chair of Forgetfulness, by the time he escaped, someone else had taken his throne. He never regained his fame and died a sad death.

While Hades did not sit atop Mount Olympus with the other Olympians, he was still viewed as a powerful god in Greek mythology. Ancient Greeks were often afraid to even say his name. But while they feared Hades, they also respected him. He wasn't seen as an angry god. He was a just god who had the difficult task of ruling the land of the dead and all who dwelt there.

GREEK GODS AND GODDESSES

Demeter—goddess of agriculture and farming. When her daughter was kidnapped into the Underworld, she stopped all plants from growing until her child was freed.

Hades—god of the Underworld and of wealth and riches. He is also a bit of a trickster and does not appreciate mortals invading his realm.

Helios—Titan god of the Sun. Helios was said to drive a golden chariot across the sky from east to west every day.

Hermes—god of many domains, including herds and flocks, travelers and hospitality, and athletics. He was most well known as the personal messenger of Zeus.

Persephone—goddess of the Underworld. Persephone was tricked by Hades into being his queen. As a compromise, she spent three months of the year in the Underworld with him and nine months on Mount Olympus with her mother, the goddess Demeter.

Poseidon—god of the sea and Zeus's brother.

Thanatos—the personification of death. Thanatos gently guided departed souls into the afterlife.

Zeus—god of the sky and ruler of the Greek gods. He was known for trying to be just and fair.

OTHER PATHS TO EXPLORE

As you have learned, mortals, heroes, and gods all had their own reasons for venturing into the Underworld. But what if they had approached their challenges differently?

1. After her daughter goes missing, Demeter confronts Zeus, rulers of the Olympian gods. What if Demeter attacked and defeated Zeus in battle? How might the world in Greek myths be different if the goddess of the harvest ruled instead of the god of the sky?

2. During Orpheus's journey into the Underworld, he sees the dome where the three judges pass judgment on the spirits of the dead. What if Orpheus went before them? What would they say of his life? How would Orpheus convince them to tell him where his wife, Eurydice, is, and how would he then get her back?

3. After Hercules releases Theseus, he has to leave his friend Pirithous behind and return to the land of the living. But what if, for one last quest, Theseus decides to return to the Underworld to rescue Pirithous? How might he help his friend escape Hades's clutches?

READ MORE

Fajardo, Anika. *Hercules and His 12 Labors: an Interactive Mythological Adventure.* North Mankato, Minn.: Capstone Press, 2017.

Hoena, Blake. *Everything Mythology.* National Geographic Kids Everything. Washington, DC: National Geographic Children's Books, 2014.

Lupton, Hugh & Daniel Morden. *Orpheus and Eurydice.* Cambridge, Mass.: Barefoot Books, 2013.

INTERNET SITES

FactHound offers a safe, fun way to find Internet sites related to this book. All of the sites on FactHound have been researched by our staff.

Here's all you do:
Visit *www.facthound.com*
Type in this code: 9781515748236

GLOSSARY

Daemon (DEE-muhn)—a spirit or supernatural being

fleece (FLEESS)—a sheep or ram's wooly hide

immortal (i-MOR-tuhl)—unable to be killed

labyrinth (LAH-brinth)—a maze of winding passages that is difficult to find the way out of

lyre (LEER)—a U-shaped stringed instrument

mortal (MOR-tuhl)—a being, such as a human, who will eventually die

oracle (OR-uh-kuhl)—a person whom a god speaks through; in myths, gods used oracles to predict the future or to tell people how to solve problems

patron (PAY-truhn)—someone who supports an artist or writer or a person named as a guardian or supporter

quest (KWEST)—a long journey to perform a task or find something

tribute (TRIB-yoot)—a payment made by one ruler or country to another as a sign of dependence

venom (VEN-uhm)—a poison produced by some animals, such as a venomous snake

BIBLIOGRAPHY

Apollodorus. *The Library (Bibliotheca)*. Theoi Classical E-Texts Library. http://www.theoi.com/Text/Apollodorus1.html

Barnett, Mary. *Gods and Myths of Ancient Greece*. New York: Modern Publishing Regency House, 1997.

Buxton, Richard. *The Complete World of Greek Mythology*. London: Thames & Hudson, Ltd., 2004.

Hesiod. *Theogony*. Theoi Classical E-Texts Library. http://www.theoi.com/Text/HesiodTheogony.html

Ovid. *Metamorphoses*. Theoi Classical E-Texts Library. http://www.theoi.com/Text/OvidMetamorphoses1.html

Stapleton, Michael. *The Illustrated Dictionary of Greek and Roman Mythology*. New York: Peter Bedrick Books, 1986.

Waterfield, Robin. The *Greek Myths: Stories of the Greek Gods and Heroes Vividly Retold*. New York: Metro Books, 2011.